INVASION OF TINIAN

1944 BATTLE FOR TINIAN IN THE MARIANA ISLANDS

DANIEL WRINN

D1361834

CONTENTS

GET YOUR FREE COPY OF WW2: SPIES, SNIPERS AND THE WORLD AT WAR

Never miss a new release by signing up for my free readers group. Learn of special offers and interesting details I find in my research. You'll also get WW2: Spies, Snipers and Tales of the World at War delivered to your inbox. (You can unsubscribe at any time.) Go to danielwrinn.com to sign up.

SCOUTING TINIAN'S BEACHES

Once the outcome of Saipan's battle was clear, the V Amphibious Corps Commanders turned their attention to the next objective: the island of Tinian. Three miles off Saipan's southwest coast and garrisoned with over nine-thousand Japanese troops. Many of the enemy combatants were veterans of the Manchurian Campaign, pummeled for over seven weeks by US Navy air and sea armadas.

The 2nd and 4th Marine Divisions, fresh from fighting on Saipan, were selected to assault Tinian. The vital question of where they would land was still undecided. There was firm support among assault planners to land on two narrow sand strips—codenamed White Beach 1 and White Beach 2—on Tinian's northwest coast. White Beach 1 was sixty yards wide, while White Beach 2 was one hundred and sixty.

Admiral Richmond Kelly Turner, overall commander of the Marianas' Expeditionary Force, was skeptical and suggested an alternative site codenamed Yellow Beach.

On July 3, 1944, Captain James Jones was put on alert for future reconnaissance of these potential landing sites. On July

9, the day Saipan was officially declared secured, Captain Jones got his orders from General Holland Smith. His men were to scout out Tinian's beaches and fortifications to determine the capacity to handle a landing force and keep it supplied.

Navy UDT (underwater demolition teams) would locate underwater obstacles and do the hydrographic work. Captain Jones chose Company A under the command of Captain Merwin Silverthorn and First Lieutenant Leo Shinn to command Company B. They rehearsed the operation off the beaches of Saipan's Magicienne Bay. On the evening of July 10, Navy and Marine units boarded the destroyer transports *Stringham* and *Gilmer* for the quick trip into the channel that separated the two islands.

At 2030 on July 10, the teams debarked in zodiac rubber boats and paddled to within five hundred yards of the beach, then swam the rest of the way in. Luckily, it was a black night, and although the moon rose at 2230, it was largely hidden by the clouds.

Yellow Beach was assigned to Silverthorn's Company A. He led eight UDT swimmers and twenty Marines ashore. They found a beach near Tinian Town flanked on each side by formidable cliffs. Several floating mines and underwater boulders barred the approach. On the beach, double-apron barbed wire had been strung.

Captain Silverthorn worked his way thirty yards inland in search of exit routes for the vehicles. Talkative Japanese workers were busy building pillboxes and entrenching blasting charges. Silverthorn spotted three Japanese sentries on the cliff overlooking the beach. Searchlights passed back and forth, scanning the beach approach, but Silverthorn and his men safely made it back to the *Stringham*. Yellow Beach as a landing site would not work.

In the northwest, the White Beaches reconnaissance was assigned to Company B. Strong currents push the rubber boats off course. The team heading for White Beach 1 was swept over a thousand yards north off course and never got ashore. The team headed for White Beach 2 wound up on White Beach 1 and reconnoitered the area. The *Gilmer* eventually picked up both parties. The following night, ten swimmers from Company A went to White Beach 2 and were successful.

Reports from the White Beaches were encouraging. The LVTs (amphibian tractors) and other vehicles could negotiate the reefs and get ashore. Troops could also clamber over the low cliffs flanking the beaches with little difficulty. Marines disembarking from the boats on the reef could wade ashore through a shallow surf. The Navy's UDT teams confirmed the Marine intelligence and reported: "no man-made underwater obstructions or mines were found."

After the reconnaissance team returned from White Beach 2, Admiral Turner withdrew his objection, and the command decision was made to use the northwestern beaches. The assault was set for July 24 at 0730.

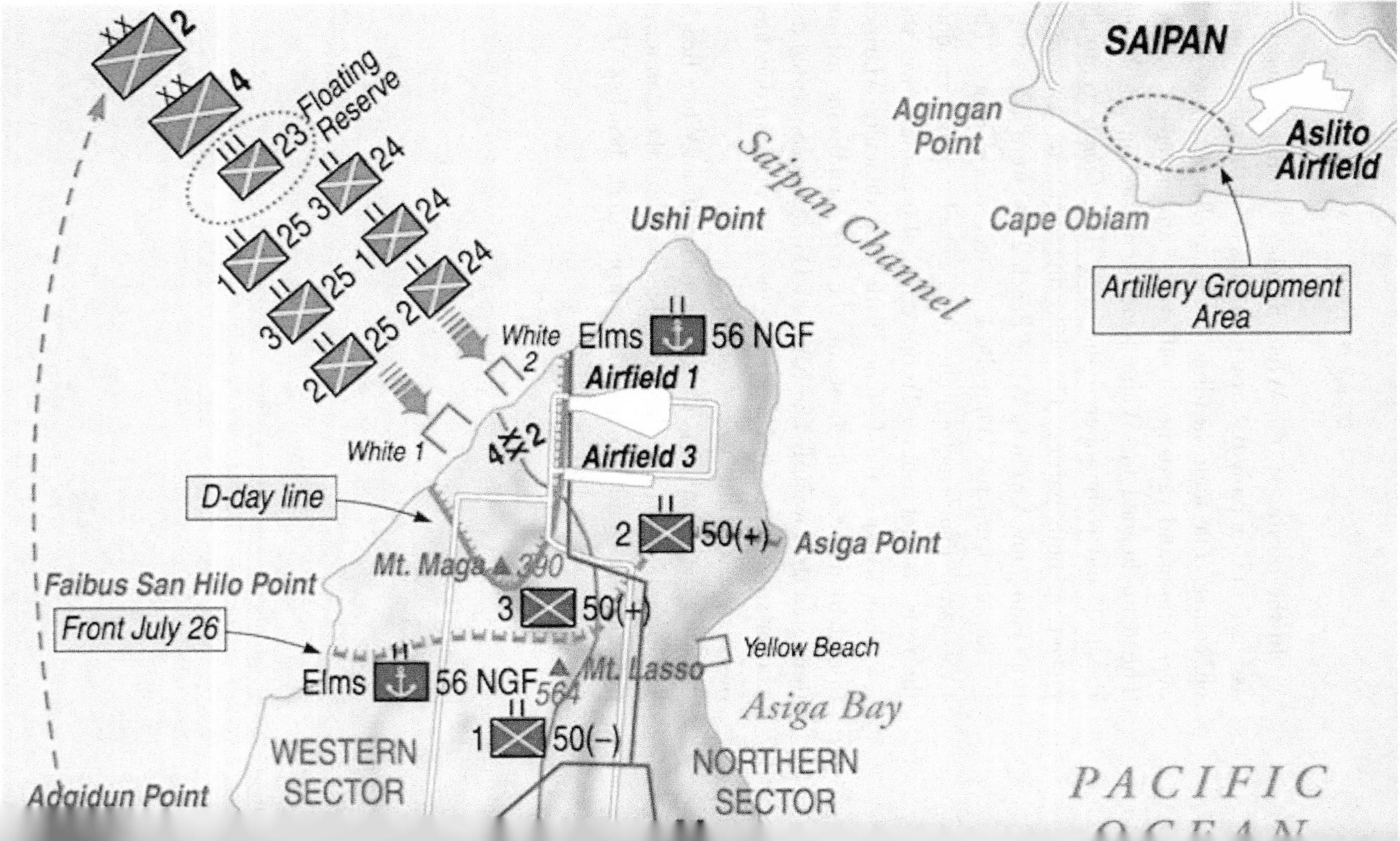

SAIPAN

Aslito Airfield

Artillery Groupment Area

Cape Obiam

Agingan Point

Saipan Channel

Ushi Point

PACIFIC OCEAN

Elms 56 NGF

Airfield 1

Airfield 3

White 2

White 1

Floating Reserve

D-day line

Faibus San Hilo Point

Front July 26

Adaidun Point

Mt. Maga 390

Mt. Tapotchau 564

Elms 56 NGF

WESTERN SECTOR

NORTHERN SECTOR

Yellow Beach

Asiga Bay

Asiga Point

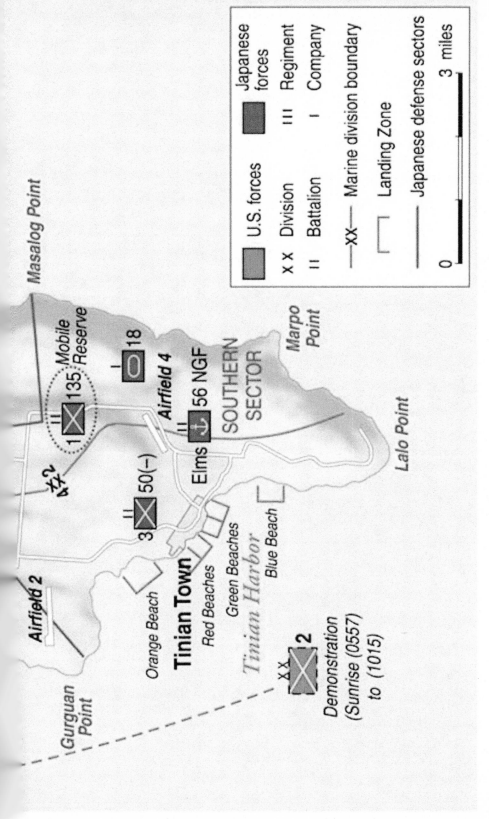

Masalog Point

Mobile Reserve

135

18

Airfield 4

56 NGF

1

SOUTHERN SECTOR

Marpo Point

XX 2

50(−)

3

Elms

Lalo Point

Airfield 2

Tinian Town

Orange Beach

Red Beaches

Green Beaches

Tinian Harbor

Blue Beach

Gurguan Point

Demonstration
(Sunrise (0557)
to (1015)

XX 2

U.S. forces

Japanese forces

X X   Division
II   Battalion
III   Regiment
I   Company

—XX— Marine division boundary
          Landing Zone
——   Japanese defense sectors

0   1   2   3 miles

PLANNING THE ASSAULT

The 2nd and 4th Marine Divisions on Saipan were tasked with seizing Tinian. The Army's 27th Infantry Division would remain on Saipan in reserve. All three had been pummeled during the Saipan campaign. Together they'd suffered more than 14,000 casualties, with over 3,200 killed in action.

This would be the fourth assault in eighteen months for the 2nd Marine Division. The division left Guadalcanal in February 1943, suffering over one thousand casualties. Another 12,000 men had diagnosed malaria cases. Eight months later, on November 20, 1943—the 2nd Marine Division had gone through one of the most intense seventy-two hours of combat in the history of island warfare at Tarawa. They endured 3,368 casualties, with just under a thousand dead.

Two and a half months before Tarawa, the division was still malaria-ridden, with troops hospitalized at a rate of over forty men a day. Ranks were filled with emaciated Marines, skin yellowed by the daily doses of the Atabrine pills. The

Saipan operation took another heavy toll on these Marines seven months later: 1,304 killed and 5,027 wounded.

The 4th Marine Division had a busy but less demanding year. They went directly into combat after their formation at Camp Pendleton. They landed on January 31, 1944, in the Marshall Islands. They suffered 787 casualties in the capture of Roi-Namur. They endured 6,025 casualties on Saipan, with more than 1,000 Marines killed. The Tinian landing would be the third assault in six months. It would also be the first under a new divisional commander—Major General Clifton Cates: a decorated World War I veteran who would later become the 19th Commandant of the Marine Corps in 1948.

"Troop morale in the Tinian operation was generally high," wrote Marine historian Carl Hoffman. "This fact takes on significance only when it's recalled the Marines had just survived a bitter month-long struggle with only a two-week lapse, and they were again ordered to assault enemy-held shores. Their spirit was more of a philosophical shrug accompanied by a 'here we go again' attitude rather than a resentment at being called upon again so soon."

The pre-invasion bombardment also helped the morale of the troops. For Jig -1 and Jig Day (Jig was the codename for D-Day on Tinian) Rear Admiral Harry Hill would command the Northern Landing Forces. He divided the island into five support sectors and assigned specific ships to each. He intended to deceive the Japanese about the true intentions of the Marine landing.

Tinian Town got the heaviest pounding the day before the landing: 2,785 rounds of 5- to 16-inch shells from battleships *Tennessee*, *Colorado*, *California*, and the cruiser *Cleveland* along with seven destroyers. *Colorado* had the best day with sixty rounds of 16-inch shells smashing the two six-inch coastal defense guns the Japanese had placed on the west near San Hilo Point—guns that could have covered the white beaches.

Due to lack of suitable targets and deception, White Beach area firing was insignificant. Naval gunfire and artillery barrages were stopped to allow massive airstrikes on railroad junctions, villages, pillboxes, cane fields, gun emplacements, and the beaches at Tinian Town. Over 350 Army and Navy planes took part in dropping over 200 rockets, 500 bombs, and thirty-four napalm bombs.

That night thirty-seven LSTs (Landing Ship, Tank) at anchor off Saipan reloaded with 4th Marine Division troops. Three days of rations, medical supplies, ammunition, water, vehicles, and other equipment were preloaded on July 15. The troops traveled light: a pair of socks, insect repellent, a spoon, emergency supplies in their pockets, and no pack on their back.

Historian Philip Crowl wrote, "I rode the ships with two transport divisions that would carry two regiments of the 2nd

Marine Division on a diversionary feint against Tinian Town and would later disembark them across the Northwestern beaches." (A similar ruse was made by the 2nd Division Marines a year later off the southeast beach of Okinawa.)

The 4th Marine Division was selected as the assault division for Tinian. The beaches were not wide enough to accommodate battalions landing abreast, much less divisions. The assault troops landed in columns—companies, platoons, and even squads.

The 2nd Division would soon follow after taking part in a feint off the beaches of Tinian Town. They hoped to tie down the main Japanese forces while the 4th Division surprised the lightly defended northern beaches.

To give the 4th Marine Division more punch after the landing, the 2nd Marine Division was stripped of some of its artillery, tank, and firepower units. They would be at the lowest strength on Tinian of any Marine division involved in an amphibious operation in all of World War II.

Even after cannibalizing from the 2nd Marine Division, the 4th would still be "skinny," wrote Lieutenant Colonel "Jumping Joe" Chambers, who commanded the 3rd Battalion 25th Regiment (3/25) Marines and later earned a Medal of Honor on Iwo Jima. The division's infantry battalion only received one replacement after the fighting on Saipan. At full strength, they averaged 880 men—at Tinian, the average strength was down by more than 35% to just over 550 men.

Due to combat fatigue, heavy losses during previous weeks and months, and under-strength units: The Marines on Tinian played a cautious game. Admiral Turner said he'd give them two weeks to seize the island. General Harry Schmidt, now in command of V Amphibious Corps, promised to get it done sooner. The island was secured after nine days. A Marine

Historian wrote, "the operation could have been finished sooner if they used more aggressive tactics." But time was no great factor—the relatively slow pace of the operation probably contributed to keeping casualties at a minimum and helped reduce troop fatigue. Tinian may have been easy on the eyes, but the heat and humidity were brutal, the cane fields were hard going, and it was monsoon season.

JIG DAY LANDING

At 0330, July 24, troop ships moved out of Saipan's Charan Kanoa harbor. They carried the 2nd and 8th Infantry Regiments of the 2nd Marine Division. This deception mission would be far bloodier than the White Beach landings and far more costly than command expected. They had a powerful escort—the battleship *Colorado*, light cruiser *Cleveland*, and destroyers *Monssen*, *Wadleigh*, *Norman Scott* and *Ramey*.

The convoy moved into Sunharon Harbor across from Tinian Town just before dawn. At 0601, the attack transport *Calvert* lowered its landing craft, and by 0630, all twenty-two of its boats were in the water. Marines climbed down cargo nets, and within thirty minutes: US planes strafed and bombed the runs, paying particular attention to Tinian Town. Rockets and shells from battleships, light and heavy cruisers, destroyers, and over thirty gunboats saturated the beaches. Massed artillery battalions in southern Saipan thundered in with 155mm rounds.

After thirty minutes, the LVCPs (Landing Craft Vehicle

Personnel, or Higgins boats) from the *Calvert* made a run toward the beach, taking on heavy artillery and mortar fire from shore. Rear Admiral Hill, trying to avoid casualties, ordered the boats to withdraw and reform. A second run followed and took on heavy fire from Japanese resistance on shore. Several of the boats were sprayed with shell fragments but continued until less than four hundred yards off the beach before turning back.

While the small boats engaged in this maneuver, the battleship *Colorado* came under fire at a range of just over 3,000 yards from two Japanese 6-inch guns near Tinian Town. These guns had gone undetected during the pre-invasion reconnaissance. Within fifteen minutes, Japanese gunners scored twenty-two direct hits on the *Colorado* and six on the destroyer *Norman Scott*. The casualties among the Marine detachments and crews were costly: 227 wounded and 69 killed. The *Colorado* limped back to Saipan. That Japanese battery survived for four entire days until finally destroyed by the battleship *Tennessee*.

The losses taken by these two ships alone exceeded those suffered by the larger Marine landing forces on the northwestern beaches. But this deception served its purpose. One battalion of the Japanese *50th Infantry Regiment* and elements of the *56th Naval Guard Force* froze in place around Tinian Town. This deception also convinced the Japanese commander Colonel Kiyochi Ogata that he had thwarted an invasion. His message to Tokyo described his forces repelled over one-hundred landing barges.

These "barges" reloaded back onto the *Calvert* at 1000. The convoy steamed north to the White Beaches, where the Marine 4th Division troops had landed after a mishap. A UDT party using floats and carrying explosives swam to White Beach 2 before dawn to blast away boulders and destroy beach mines. But a squall caused this mission to fail. Now the floats were scattered and explosives lost. The Marines would pay a heavy price for this aborted mission a few hours later.

To offset the UDT mission's failure, airstrikes were ordered at 0630. Observers claimed that five of the fourteen known beach mines had been destroyed. One battery of 155mm "Long Tom" guns on Saipan fired smoke shells at the Japanese command post on Mount Lasso. They also laid smoke in the woods, the bluffs, and beaches to hinder Japanese observation.

The 24th Marines were tasked with assaulting White Beach 1 while White Beach 2 went to the 25th Marines. Almost at once, two battalions of the 25th Marines loaded into sixteen LVTs and landed in columns of companies on White Beach 2. The 2nd Battalion was on the right and the 3rd Battalion on the left.

Units of the 24th Marines loaded into twenty-five LVTs and crossed the line of departure 3,500 yards offshore at 0715. Ahead of them were LCIs (landing craft, infantry) and a company of the 2nd Armored Amphibian Battalion. They raked the beaches with barrage rockets and automatic cannon fire. In the twenty-five-minute run to the beach, the trip-laden LVTs took scattered small arms and machine-gun fire.

At White Beach 1, a small Japanese beach detachment holed up in caves and crevices put up a fierce resistance with small arms fire. Company E gunners quickly destroyed them.

In less than an hour, the entire 1st and 2nd Battalions of the 24th Marines were ashore on White Beach 1 and prepared to move inland. The 2nd Battalion faced erratic small arms, mortar, and artillery fire during the first few hundred yards of its advance. After that, the battalion had an easy walk for the rest of the day, gaining their O-1 line objective by 1600. They also occupied the western edge of Airfield 3 and cut the main road that linked Airfield 1 with the eastern coast and southern Tinian. Still receiving sporadic small-arms fire, the battalion dug in for the night.

On the left flank, heavy fire stalled the 1st Battalion. Enemy shooters hid in patches of vegetation and cave positions. Flamethrower tanks were set up against these positions, but the Japanese kept up a stiff resistance. As a result, the 1st Battalion did not reach their objective—400 yards short of their objective by the afternoon. This left a gap between the two perimeters. The regimental 3rd Battalion waiting in reserve was called up.

The 25th Regiment ran into problems. The beach in the surrounding area had been seeded with mines that the UDT teams and offshore gunners failed to destroy. It took five hours to clear them out. Three LVTs and a jeep were destroyed in the process. Several booby traps were left for the Marines to deal with: Cases of beer and watches wired to explode in the hands of careless souvenir hunters.

Inland, troops from Ogata's *50th Infantry Regiment* put up a vigorous defense with mortars, anti-boat and anti-tank guns, and other automatic weapons placed in fortified ravines, pill-boxes, caves and field entrenchments. A pair of 47mm guns kept Marines on the defensive. After they finally bypassed the difficult positions, they left fifty dead Japanese in the gun pits.

Colonel Chambers, the 3/25 Marines commander, later wrote of the confusion on the beach, "the confusion you always get when you land, and trying to reorganize under fire." One of his company commanders was killed fifteen minutes after landing. It took a while to get a replacement on scene and up to speed. Then there was still the problem of mines and artillery fire from the Japanese command post on Mount Lasso, less than two miles away.

By late afternoon Colonel Chambers' battalion had reached its objective of 1,500 yards inland to the center of the line and had tied the 24th onto its left flank. Other battalions of the 25th came up short of their O-1 line. This created a crescent-shaped beachhead that was 3,500 yards wide at the shoreline and bulged inland 1,500 yards at sunset.

But the day's greatest confusion came from the 23rd Marines. The regiment had been waiting on LSTs in division reserve during the landing. At 0740, troops were ordered to board LVTs parked cheek to jowl in the tank decks. Their engines were running and spewing carbon monoxide. After thirty minutes, the cooped-up troops developed headaches, got nauseous, and started vomiting.

Colonel Louis Jones ordered the men to unload and return topside until a launch order was finally received at 1030. The regiment debarked and eventually got ashore at 1400 despite an incredible series of communication breakdowns, where

Colonel Jones at crucial times, was out of touch with his battalions and divisions.

Besides disrupted radio communications, Colonel Jones was stuck in an LVT with a bad engine. He waited seven hours to get ashore with his staff, leading to a division complaint about his regiment's tardiness. Command noted that "fortunately no serious harm was done by the delay."

But at the end of the operation, Colonel Jones left the division. He was promoted to brigadier general and assigned a position as assistant division commander of the 1st Marine Division leading up to the Okinawa landings.

A similar problem happened involving the 2nd Marine Division. After the feint at Tinian Town, the division sailed north and waited offshore of the White Beaches throughout the day. At 1530, the landing force commander, General Harry Schmidt, ordered a battalion from the 8th Marines to land on White Beach, backing up the 24th Marines. General Schmidt wanted a battalion ashore by 1600.

Because of the poor communications and transport confusion, the deadline was missed. It wasn't until 2100 when the unit entered into its log, "Dug in in assigned position."

But while all the details weren't perfect, the overall operation had gone well in the morning and afternoon. By the standards of Saipan and Tarawa, casualties were light—225 wounded and 15 dead. The Japanese body count was over 435 men.

Despite narrow beaches, undiscovered mines, and drizzling rain, over 15,500 troops were still put ashore. Along with massive quantities of equipment and material, including four artillery battalions, twenty-four half-tracks with 75mm guns. Forty-eight medium and fifteen flamethrower tanks, which found the Tinian terrain agreeable for tank operations.

Tanks got into action early that morning and led the 24th

in tank-infantry attacks. They'd also come to the aid of the 23rd Marines as the regiment moved inland to take over the division's right flank. Despite some units failing to reach their first objectives, the beachhead was large and extended inland nearly a mile and embraced defensible territory.

Not bad for a day's work.

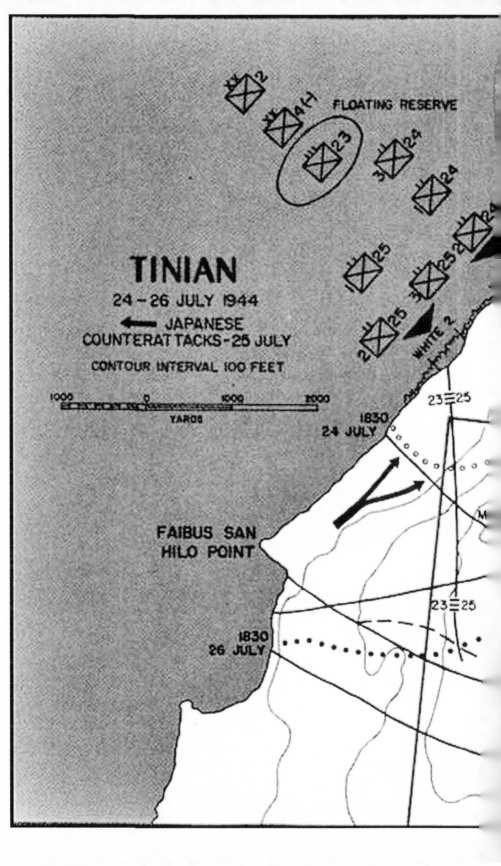

FLOATING RESERVE

TINIAN

24 – 26 JULY 1944

← JAPANESE COUNTERATTACKS – 25 JULY

CONTOUR INTERVAL 100 FEET

1000   0   1000   2000
YARDS

WHITE 2

1830
24 JULY

23 ≡ 25

FAIBUS SAN
HILO POINT

23 ≡ 25

1830
26 JULY

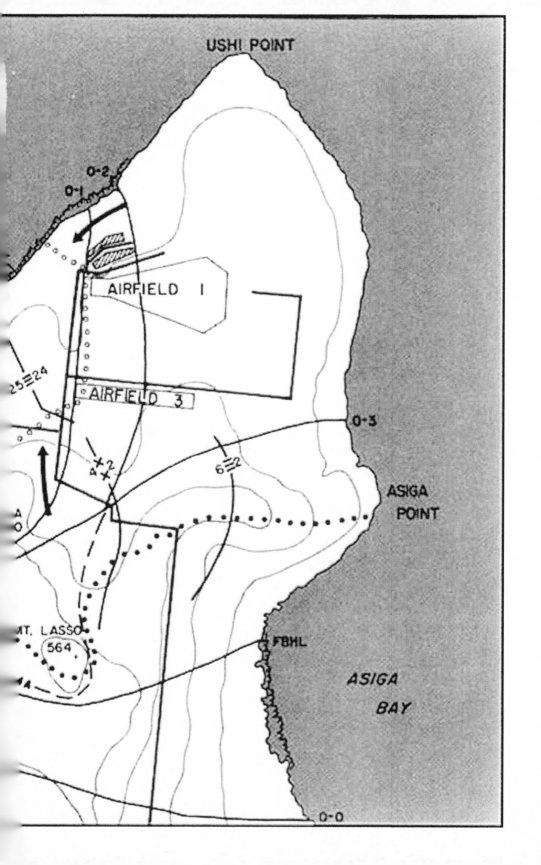

JAPANESE COUNTERATTACK

At 1630, General Clifton B. Cates, in command of the 4th Marine Division, ordered his forces to button up for the night. Command expected a nighttime counterattack. Barbed wire, preloaded on amphibian vehicles, was strung along the front.

Stockpiled ammunition could be seen in every weapons position. Machine guns were emplaced to allow interlocking fields of fire. Target areas were assigned to mortar crews. Artillery batteries in the rear were pre-registered to hit enemy approach routes and fire illumination shells to light up the battlefield. Anti-tank 37mm guns with canister ammunition (antipersonnel shells firing large pellets for close infighting) were positioned upfront. This would ensure severe casualties and do the greatest damage to the enemy.

The Marines dug in and waited for whatever the night would bring. The 24th Marines were backed up by the 1/8 Marines, occupying the northern half of the crescent defense. The 25th with a battalion of the 23rd occupied the southern half of the crescent. The rest of the 23rd were in reserve, along with artillery battalions from the 10th and 14th Marines, waiting in the rear on high alert.

The Japanese prepared for their counterattack. Because of their shattered communication lines, it would not be a coordinated operation. Units would need to act independently. Colonel Ogata issued a general order on June 28: "destroy the enemy on beaches with one blow. Especially where time prevents quick movement of forces within the island."

The Japanese had 850 naval troops at the Ushi Point airfields on the Marines' northern flank. Opposite the center of the Marine lines, near Mount Lasso, were another two battalions of the *50th Infantry Regiment* and a tank company of 1,500 Japanese troops in total. On the west coast facing the Marines' right flank were another 250 men from an infantry company of the *50th Regiment*—along with an anti-tank squad and an anti-tank detachment.

The Japanese *Mobile Counterattack Force*—a 750-man battalion of the *135th Infantry Regiment*, equipped with new rifles and demolition charges, waited six miles from the White Beaches.

Japanese movement toward the northwestern beaches within the Marine lines was treacherous. All daylight movement was closely monitored by air surveillance and vulnerable to American firepower.

But the battalion set out under its commander, Captain Izumi, and was hit frequently by unobserved artillery and naval gunfire. Izumi advanced and made his objective through skillful use of terrain for concealment. At 2230 he probed the center of the Marine lines where the 2/24 Marines were tied in with the 3rd Battalion.

According to a Marine Combat correspondent: "While most of the Japanese crept along forward of the lines, a two-man reconnaissance detail climbed up on a battered building forward of the 24th Marines and audaciously jotted notes or drew sketches of the front lines. When Marines recognized this impudent gesture, they rewarded them with a thundering concentration of artillery fire."

Another Marine wrote of his vivid memory that night: "A big gully ran from southeast to northwest into the western edge of our area. Anyone in their right mind would have figured that if there were going to be any counterattacks—they'd come from that gully.

"Throughout the night, Marines reported they heard a lot of Japanese chatter from down in the gully. Then they hit us at about midnight in K Company's area. They hauled a couple of 75mm howitzers by hand with them, and when they got up to where they could fire at us—they hit us hard. I believe K Company did a damn good job, but about two-hundred Japs pushed through us [1,500 yards] to the beach area.

"Once the Japs hit the rear areas, all the artillery and machine guns started shooting like hell. Fire came in from the rear and grazed right up over our heads. During this, the enemy that hit Company L was putting up one hell of a fight about seventy-five yards from where I was—and there wasn't a damn thing I could do about it.

"Over in Company K's area is where the attack really developed. That was where Lieutenant McGuire and his 37mm guns on the left flank were firing canister. I watched two Marines manning a machine gun layout a cone of dead Jap bodies in front of them. A dead Jap officer laid right in there with them."

A Combat Marine correspondent later described this action: "Marines held their fire until the Japanese were less than a thousand yards away—then they opened up. The Japanese charged. Screaming '*banzai*' and firing machine guns and throwing grenades. It was near impossible for the Marines to hold on and continue firing. The next morning, we counted the Jap bodies piled in front of us. Over 250 dead Japanese soldiers.

"Just before sunrise, two tank companies showed up. They wanted to get right at the Japs and were sent off to an area held by Companies L and K. The major returned in less than fifteen minutes and said, 'you don't need tanks. You need undertakers. I've never seen so many dead Japs.'"

Another large party of Japanese troops was *stacked up* by the 75mm howitzer gunners of the 14th Marines supported by the 50-caliber machine guns of batteries E and F. These machine guns literally tore the Japanese to pieces. Over 600 Japanese were killed in their suicidal attack on the Marine center.

On the left flank, the 1/24 Marines came under attack at 0200 from 550 *Special Naval Landing Force* troops out of the barracks at the Ushi Point airfields. Company A was hit so hard it was at one point reduced to only 30 men with weapons. Company A was forced to draw reinforcements from corpsmen, engineers, communicators, and members of the shore party.

Illumination flares soared over the battlefield. This allowed Marines to use 37mm canister shells, mortars, and machine-gun fire to good effect. The fight continued until dawn, when medium tanks from the 4th Tank Battalion lumbered up to break up the last attacking Japanese troops. By this point, many Japanese had used their grenades to commit suicide.

As the sun rose, 470 Japanese bodies were counted in the defensive crescent, mostly in front of Company A's position.

The last enemy attack that night hit the right flank of the Marines at 0330. A handful of Japanese tanks rattled up from Tinian Town's direction to attack the 23rd Marines' position. They were met with fierce fire from anti-tank guns, Marine artillery, small arms, and bazookas.

Lieutenant Jim Lucas was a professional reporter who enlisted in the Marine Corps after the attack on Pearl Harbor and was commissioned in the field. He later wrote: "Three lead tanks broke through the wall of fire. One glowed a blood-red and turned crazily on its tracks before careening into a ditch. A second, mortally wounded, turned its machine guns on its tormentors, firing into the ditches in one last desperate effort to fight its way free. After another hundred yards, it stopped dead in its tracks.

"The third tank tried frantically to turn around and retreat, but our boys closed in and literally blasted it apart. Bazookas knocked out a fourth tank, killing the driver. The rest of the crew piled out of the turret screaming. The fifth tank was now surrounded and tried to flee. Our bazookas made quick work of it. Another hit set it on fire, and its crew was cremated.

"The sixth tank was chased off by a Marine driving a Jeep. But destroying these tanks did not end the fight on the right flank. Infantry from the Japanese *50th Regiment* continued to attack the 2/23 Marines. While they were repulsed and killed in large numbers, mainly through effective use of anti-tank 37mm guns with canister shot. In the last hopeless moments of the assault, some wounded Japanese destroyed themselves by detonating a magnetic tank mine, producing a horrific blast."

From a Japanese standpoint, that night's work was a disaster. Over 1,200 bodies were left on the battlefield: several hundred more carted away during the night. With fewer than one hundred Marines wounded or killed, losing these Japanese troops broke the back of the already poor defenses of Tinian. Now that their communications were shattered by sustained fire from Saipan and increasing fire from Tinian, survivors were capable of only the weakest, most dazed sort of resistance. During the next seven days, small groups of Japanese took advantage of the darkness to launch night attacks, but mostly, they only withdrew in no particular order until there was nowhere left for them to withdraw.

Most agreed that the battle for Tinian was over. But 4th Division intelligence officer Colonel Gooderham McCormick, a Marine reserve officer, later to become the mayor of Philadelphia, did not agree: "we believed after the counterattack the enemy was capable of a still harder fight. And from day-to-day during our advance expected an even more bitter fight that never materialized."

Hard work still lay ahead. A demanding task was the exhausting but straightforward job of humping through the cane fields and humidity with frequent monsoon downpours. Fearful of not only sniper fire, booby traps and mines but also fires that could sweep through the cane fields and incinerate anyone caught in its path.

PEOPLE SHOOTING GROUSE

Colonel "Bucky" Buchanan was an assistant naval gunfire officer for the 4th Division at Tinian. He wrote of his experiences: "We fought the same way at Tinian that we did on Saipan. It was a handholding, linear operation, like a bunch of bush beaters, people shooting grouse or something. The idea was to flush out every Jap consistently as we go down rather than driving down the main road with a fork and cutting this and that off in what I called creative tactics. This was the easiest and safest thing to do. Who can criticize it? We were successful. And again, what little resistance was left was pushed into the edge of the island—and quickly destroyed."

The grouse shooting metaphor was simple, but even the 4th Division commander, General Cates thought the campaign had a sporting aspect. "The fighting was different from most any that we'd experienced because it was good terrain. A good, clean operation the men really enjoyed."

Before the bush beating could begin in a proper order, three things needed to happen. First, the 2nd Division needed to be put ashore. This was completed on the morning of July 26.

Next, Japanese pockets of resistance and stragglers on the island's northern sector had to be crushed. That job was completed on the 26th as the 2nd Marine Division swept across Ushi Point airfields and reached the east coast before turning south.

The 4th Division seized Mount Maga in the center of the island, also on the 26th. This forced Colonel Ogata and his staff to abandon their command post on Mount Lasso, which fell to the Marines without a struggle. Two days later, Navy Seabees had the Ushi Point airfields in operation for Army P-47 Thunderbolt Fighters.

The third objective was to drive south a skirmish line of infantry and tanks stretching across the 29 square mile island. This was also accomplished on the 26th. The 4th Division lined up in the western half of the island. The 23rd Marines were on the coast, with the 24th in the center and the 25th on the left flank. The 2nd Division lined up with the 2nd Marines on the east coast with the 6th Marines in the center now all tied into the 25th. The 8th Marines stayed in the north to mop up any further resistance.

This was achieved with only minor casualties. On July 26, Jig Day+2, the 2nd Division reported two dead and 14 wounded. These were the heaviest losses since the first day and night of fighting had been sustained by the 14th Marines, the 4th Division's artillery regiment, following the Japanese counterattack. An enemy shell smashed into the 1st Battalion's fire direction center, killing the battalion commander, intelligence officer, ops officer, and seven other staff members. Fourteen Marines in the battalion headquarters were also wounded. Nearly all the casualties sustained by the regiment during the Tinian campaign happened on that one day—July 25.

The morning of July 27, Jig Day+3, started the bush beating drive to the south. General Schmidt's plan for the first two days of the drive alternated between the two divisions' main thrust. The official history of the operation likens it to "a man elbowing his way through the crowd swinging on one arm then the other."

The 2nd Division got the heavier work on July 27. Artillery firing from southern Saipan had softened up suspected enemy positions early in the morning. At 0730, the 2nd Division began its advance. They advanced swiftly and were harassed by sporadic arms fire. By 1345 they'd reached their objective. They gained over 4,000 yards in less than six hours.

The 4th Division moved out late in the morning against "negligible opposition" and reached their objective by noon before calling it a day. A Japanese prisoner of war complained to his captors, "you couldn't drop a stick without bringing down artillery."

On the morning of July 28, the 4th Marines got the "swinging elbow" job. It was now apparent the remaining

Japanese defenders were fleeing to the hills and caves along the southern coast. The opposition to the Marine advance was virtually nil. The 4th Marines moved more than two miles in less than four hours, with troops riding in half-tracks and tanks.

Starting again early in the afternoon in a *blitz* fashion, they overran the airfield at Gurguan Point before quitting for the day at 1730 after gaining just over 7000 yards—a little over 4 miles. The 2nd Division got light-duty and moved ahead a few hundred yards, reaching their objective in two hours, and digging in to wait for the next morning.

General Cates later wrote how he spurred on his 4th Division troops: "'Look men,' I said. 'The Hawaiian island of Maui is waiting for us. See the ships out there? The quicker you get this over with, the quicker we'll be back there.' They almost ran to the other end of that island."

On the 29th, General Schmidt dropped the elbowing tactic and ordered both divisions to move as far and as fast as sensible. Opposition had been so light that preparatory fires were canceled to save the dwindling artillery supply shells left on Saipan and to prevent any "waste of naval gunfire on areas largely deserted by the enemy."

While the 2nd Marines in the eastern terrain ran into pockets of resistance at Masalog Point, the 6th Marines encountered a twenty-man Japanese patrol attempting to penetrate the regiment's lines after dark. The 25th took heavy sniper fire as they moved through cane fields and engaged in a heavy firefight with Japanese troops fighting from dug-in positions later in the day. The Marines suffered casualties and one of their tanks was disabled in the fight. But the resistance was eventually overcome. The 24th Marines operating near the west coast ran into Japanese positions, including a series of mutually supporting bunkers. The 4th Tank Battalion reported that the area had to be overrun twice by tanks before the resistance ended.

By nightfall, more than half of Tinian was in Marine hands. The 4th Division Marines could see Tinian Town from their foxholes. While great for morale, the night was spoiled by weather and heavy enemy activity. A soaking rain poured through the night. Enemy mortars and artillery fired relentlessly, drawing counter-battery fire from Marine gunners. Mortars and small arms fire silenced probes in front of the 3/25 Marines—forty Japanese bodies were found in the area at dawn.

On July 30 (Jig Day+6), Tinian Town became the principal objective of the 4th Division. At 0730, all of the division's artillery battalions laid down preparatory fire in front of Marine lines. After ten minutes, the firing stopped, and the troops moved out. At once, two destroyers and a cruiser lying in Sunharon Harbor of Tinian Town started an hour-long bombardment to support the Marines. The 1/24 Marines advanced 600 yards before coming under heavy fire from the caves along the coast north of town.

With the help of tanks and armored amphibians operating offshore, this problem was solved. Flame-throwing tanks worked over the caves, allowing engineers to seal them with demolition charges. A 75mm gun hidden in one cave was found and destroyed.

The regiment entered the ruins of Tinian Town at 1430. Except for a lone Japanese soldier—eliminated on the spot— the town was deserted. After searching through the rubble for snipers and documents, Marines advanced to their O-7 line objective south of town. The greatest danger was from mines and booby traps planted in beach areas and roads.

As the 24th continued south, the 25th Marines seized Airfield 4 on the outskirts of Tinian Town. A Japanese prisoner revealed that the unfinished airfield was rushed to completion in order to accommodate relief planes promised by Tokyo. Only one plane was parked on the crushed coral airstrip—a lone Zero fighter. Flying suits, goggles, and other equipment were found in the supply room.

En route to the airfield, the 25th took light small arms fire and while crossing the airstrip, was mortared from positions in the south. This was the 25th's last action in the Tinian campaign. They went into reserve and were relieved by units of the 23rd and the 1/8 Marines.

The 2nd Division operating east of the 4th ran into intermittent opposition from machine gun positions and a 70mm howitzer. The 3/2 Marines of the 2nd Division had the roughest time. After they silenced the howitzer, they attacked across an open field and chased a Japanese force into a large cave. With the help of a flame-throwing tank, ninety-three Japanese were killed, and four machine guns destroyed.

Afterward, the battalion came under mortar fire. The unit commander, Colonel Walter Layer wrote: "It was beyond my memory as to the number of casualties the 3rd suffered at that time. I remember rendering first aid to wounded Marines and seeing seven wounded or killed by enemy mortar fire. Half-tracks and tanks took the enemy under fire, destroying enemy mortars."

There were more minor delays, but the division reached the objective on time and dug-in by 1830. Nearly eighty percent of the island was now in American hands.

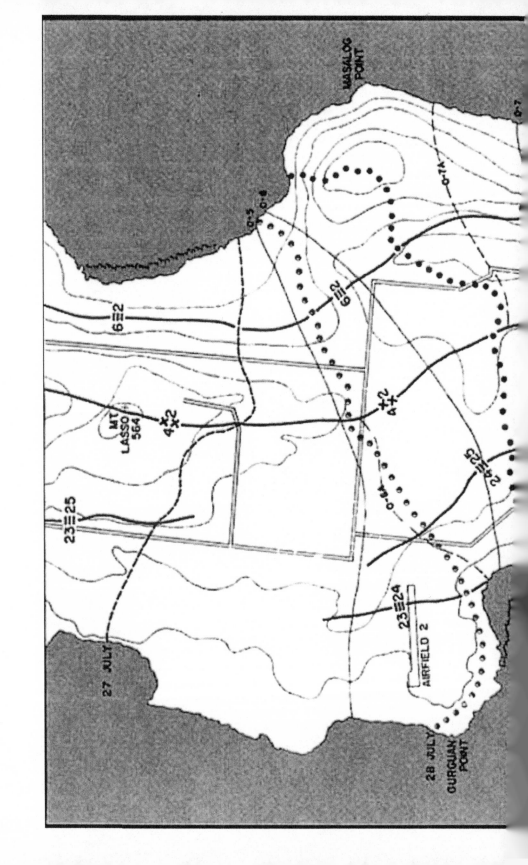

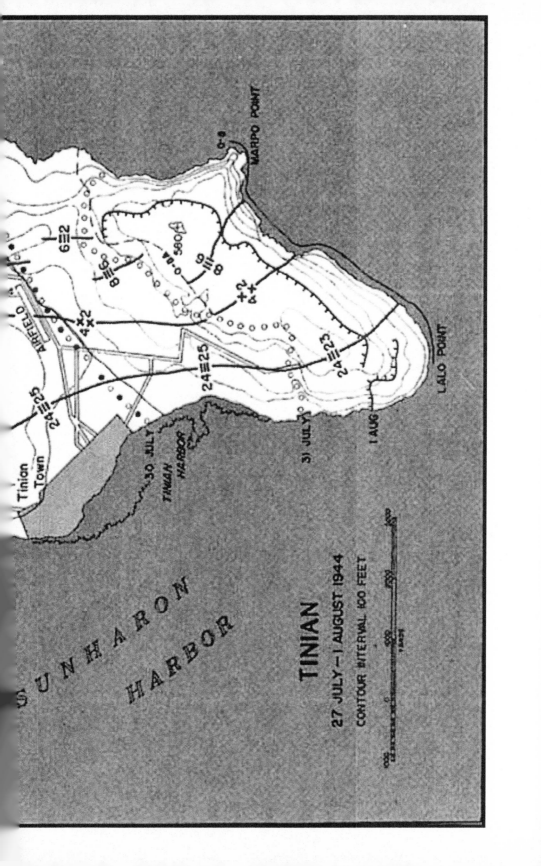

TINIAN

27 JULY – 1 AUGUST 1944

CONTOUR INTERVAL 100 FEET

SUNHARON HARBOR

MARPO POINT

LALO POINT

Tinian Town

TINIAN HARBOR

AIRFIELD

30 JULY

31 JULY

1 AUG

END OF RESISTANCE

The Japanese were now confined to a small area of south-eastern Tinian. Marines had advanced so quickly that only four miles of the island remained safe firing for ships not supporting battalions.

General Schmidt saw the end in sight in the late afternoon of July 30. He ordered the divisions to drive all the way to the southeast coastline and seize all territory remaining in enemy hands and destroy any Japanese troops.

This was not an insignificant assignment and caused the heaviest fighting since the Jig-Day counterattack. A Japanese officer captured on July 29 estimated that 500 troops of the *56th Naval Guard Force* and 2,000 troops of the *50th Infantry Regiment* were in battle-ready condition in the island's southeastern area. US intelligence estimated on July 29, based on daily reports from the divisions, that 2,800 Japanese troops had already been killed or taken prisoner up to that point. If this was true, then nearly two-thirds of the 9,000 Japanese defenders would still be alive and ready to defend the island.

The main Japanese force occupied rugged terrain that was difficult to reach and traverse—well suited for their defensive purposes. Outside of Tinian Town, the gentle landscape ended with the ground rising to plateaus of over 5,000 feet long and 2,000 yards wide—with altitudes over 500 feet. There were many caves. The plateaus were rocky and covered with thick brush. All along the east coast, cliff walls rose and seemed impossible to scale. Cliffs and jungle growth obstructed the approaches. The road in the center of the plateau led to its top and was reportedly mined. This plateau would be the last hold out for the remaining Japanese.

Next came the most intense bombardment any Japanese force had yet experienced in World War II. Marine artillery regiments on southern Saipan fired throughout the night of July 30 into the wooded cliff lines. Battleships *California* and *Tennessee* along with the heavy cruiser *Louisville* and light cruisers *Birmingham* and *Montpelier* began two sustained bombardments at 0600.

Firing for over an hour, they stopped to allow a forty-minute strike by 126 P-47 Thunderbolt Fighters, Mitchell Bombers, and Grumman Avenger Bombers from the carrier

Kitkun Bay. These planes dropped seventy tons of explosives before the offshore gunfire resumed for another thirty minutes.

The battleships and cruisers fired over 600 tons of shells at their targets. The 10th and 14th Marines' artillerymen and gunners fired over 7,000 rounds during the night. According to a Japanese prisoner, the effect was "unbearable."

The following day, the 2nd Marines' task was to clear out the western coastal area with one battalion assigned for the plateau's seizure. The 2nd Marines intended to seal off the east coast at the base of the plateau. The 6th, 8th, and 23rd Marines would assault the cliff areas and advance to the top of the plateau.

The 24th Marines jumped off at 0830 and advanced into the coastal plains. They immediately encountered brush and undergrowth so dense that tank operations would be hampered. Armored amphibians lying offshore fired against enemy beach positions and covered the regiment's right flank as they made their way down the coast. A platoon-sized Japanese beach unit launched a foolish counterattack on the 1/24 Marines at 0950. The Japanese were destroyed. Flame throwing tanks burned off brush and undergrowth, which concealed the Japanese riflemens' positions.

The 3rd Battalion on the regiment's left flank assaulted the base of the plateau. They encountered minimal opposition until 1610 when they took machine gun and rifle fire from cliff positions. Tanks were called up but got caught in a minefield and were delayed for several hours while engineers cleared dozens of mines.

The 1/23 Marines encountered a similar problem. As the regiment approached the plateau, they ran into intense small arms fire from two positions. A small village at the base of the cliff and from the cliff face itself. They took fire from a "large caliber weapon." Marines pressed forward without tank support, running a few yards, then diving, and getting up to advance again. Marine tanks finally came in search of this elusive and well-concealed weapon. One tank took six hits from the Japanese gun. A second tank was hit, but in the process, a concrete camouflage bunker hiding a 47mm anti-tank gun and twenty enemy troops was destroyed.

The 2/23 Marines came under fire from machine gunners and riflemen. One of their supporting tanks was disabled by a mine. Its crew was taken to safety by another tank, but the disabled tank was taken over by the Japanese and used as an armored machine gun nest. Other tanks were dispatched to take it out. The 23rd Regiment also lost two 37mm guns and a 1-ton truck belonging to the regiment's half-track platoon. The guns and the vehicle got too far ahead and came under heavy fire before being abandoned. The platoon later retrieved one of the guns and removed the breech block from the other. The 50-caliber machine gun from its truck mounting was brought back.

By late afternoon, the 1/23 Marines got a foothold on top of the plateau. The 3rd Battalion soon followed. On their left flank, the 3/8 Marines shrugged off small arms fire to reach the cliff's base where they were delayed for the night. The 1st Battalion had better luck. Company A made it to the top of the plateau at 1630 and was soon followed by the entire battalion and Companies E and G from the 2/8 Marines.

Captain Carl Hoffman commander of Company G of the 2/8 Marines later wrote a definitive history of the Saipan and Tinian campaigns. In an interview, he described his own experiences on top of the plateau on the night of July 31: "By the time we got up there, there was enough daylight to get ourselves properly barbed wired in, get our fields of fire established, and site our interlocking bands of machine gun fire. All things necessary for preparing a good defense.

"By dusk the enemy started a series of probing attacks. Some Japs made it into our positions. It was such a black night that the Japs moving around in our positions made our troops edgy and they challenged everyone in sight. We didn't have any unfortunate incidents of Marines firing on Marines because we were all well-seasoned by this point.

"While the night wore on, the intensity of enemy attacks started to build and finally they launched a full-on banzai attack against our battalion. The strange thing the Japs did here was that they executed one wave attack after another against a 37mm firing canister ammunition. That gun just stacked up dead Japanese. As soon as one gunner dropped another took his place. [Eight out of the ten Marines manning that gun were killed or wounded.] We were shoulder high with dead Japs in front of that weapon. By the next morning, we had defeated the enemy. Around us were a lot of dead ones—hundreds of them. From then on, we were able to finish the rest of the campaign without any difficulty. People often said that the Tinian campaign was the easiest campaign—in the Pacific."

Marines in that 37mm position on the escarpment might disagree with that assessment and think Tinian was the busiest campaign in the Pacific War.

Captain Hoffman had another vivid experience before leaving the island. He was obsessed with trumpets and carried his horn with him throughout the Pacific War: "On Tinian, I didn't take any chances sending my horn ashore in a battalion ambulance or a machine gun cart. I had it flown to me. One night my troops were in a small perimeter with barbed wire all around us on top of a cliff. My Marines were shouting requests: 'Pretty Baby' and 'Oh You Beautiful Doll' among others. While I was playing these tunes, all of a sudden, I heard the scream of *banzai*. One Jap soldier charged right toward me through the barbed wire. Marines had their weapons ready, and he must've been hit from fourteen different directions at once. He didn't even get to throw his grenade. He must not have liked my music. Not a supporter of my trumpet playing. But I continued with my little concert after we accounted for him."

In the early morning of August 1, a final banzai attack happened. A 150-man Japanese force attacked the 1/20 Marines on Hoffman's left flank. After twenty minutes, the attack's thrust was spent and at dawn, the Japanese withdrew. One-hundred mangled Japanese bodies laid in an area seventy yards in front of Company E from the 2/28 Marines. That night the 8th Marines took seventy-five casualties.

The next day the two divisions got back to work. The 2nd Division moved across the plateau toward the eastern cliffs. The 4th Division advanced toward the cliffs to the south and west. When they reached the edge of the escarpment and overlooked the ocean, their job was primarily done. At 1900, General Schmidt declared the island secured. This meant the organized resistance had ended. But not the killing. Hundreds of Japanese troops remained holed up in caves on the southern cliffs rising from the ocean.

On August 2, a Japanese force of 200 men charged and attacked the 3/6 Marines. After over two hours of combat, 119 Japanese were destroyed. This kind of contact continued for months. By the end of the year, the 8th Marines left on Tinian for mop-up operations had suffered sixty-seven casualties, with twenty-two Marines killed. Japanese losses were over 500 killed.

Beginning on August 1, there were large-scale surrenders by civilians fleeing the caves where they took refuge. Marine intelligence estimated that nearly 10,000 civilians were hiding in the southeast sector.

Marine General James Underhill took command of the island as military governor on August 10. He was responsible for the care and feeding of civilians. He wrote of his experiences: "Five hundred came through immediately, the next day eight hundred then one thousand, and then two thousand and so on. Numbers increased until we counted over 8,000. Another 3,000 hid in the caves and dribbled in over a period of months. It was 30 percent adult males, 20 percent adult females, and the rest were children. They were in terrible shape—hungry, sick, wounded. They had few possessions beyond the clothes on their backs.

"We estimate 4,000 civilians were killed in the bombardment of Tinian and the fighting on the island. On Saipan, Marines were helpless to prevent mass suicides among the civilian population. While we were more successful on Tinian, unfortunate incidents did occur. Civilians, for example, died under Marine fire after wandering into the lines at night."

Reports of suicides and ritual murders were common. This was taken from a report on August 3: "Several freak accidents occurred during the day. Japanese children were thrown by their parents over a cliff into the ocean. Japanese military grouped civilians in numbers of twenty and attached explosive charges to them, blowing them to bits. Both military and civilians lined up on the cliffs and hurled themselves into the ocean. Japanese soldiers pushed civilians over the cliff."

Some efforts to prevent these types of incidents were successful. Marines used amplifiers on land and offshore, promising good treatment to civilians and soldiers who would peacefully surrender. Many civilians, clad in colorful Japanese silk, responded to Marine promises, but it was plain from the expression on their faces that they expected the worst.

clean and rocky coast of the coral boulders where they'd gone ashore. He thought of the forbidding coast of Japan—the coast that could have awaited them in the fall. He said, "Tinian was a pretty good investment, I guess."

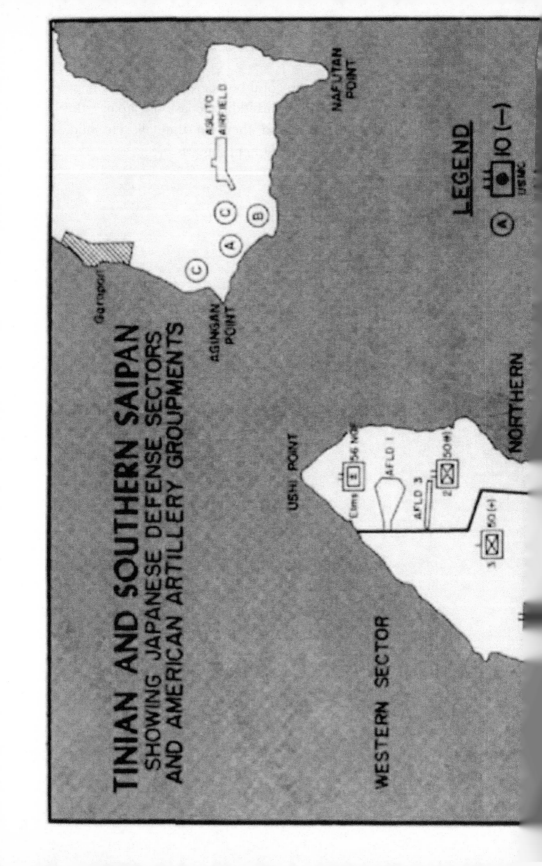

TINIAN AND SOUTHERN SAIPAN
SHOWING JAPANESE DEFENSE SECTORS
AND AMERICAN ARTILLERY GROUPMENTS

Garapan

ASLITO AIRFIELD

NAFUTAN POINT

AGINGAN POINT

Ⓒ Ⓐ Ⓒ

Ⓑ

USHI POINT

56 NGF

AFLD 1

AFLD 3

NORTHERN

WESTERN SECTOR

LEGEND

Ⓐ IO (—)
USMC

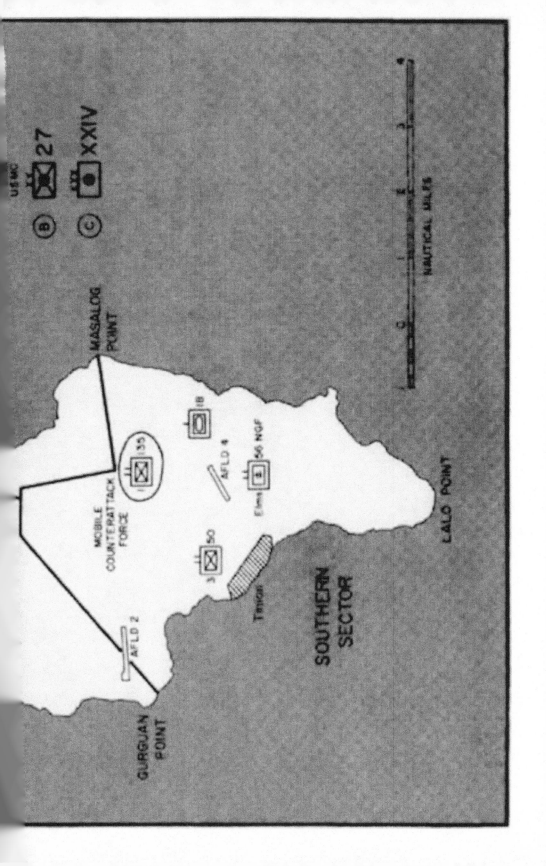

USMC

B   27

C   XXIV

MASALOG POINT

MOBILE COUNTERATTACK FORCE

135

18

AFLD 4

56 NGF

Elms

3 50

Tinian

AFLD 2

GURGUAN POINT

LALO POINT

SOUTHERN SECTOR

NAUTICAL MILES

0   1   2   3

JAPANESE DEFENSE FORCE

The Japanese fortified Tinian and other islands in the Mariana's chain in direct violation of the League of Nation's Mandate. By 1944 the Tinian garrison numbered over 9,000 Navy and Army personnel and brought the island's total population to over 25,000.

The principal fighting force was the *50th Infantry Regiment*, a detachment from the *29th Division* on Guam. Stationed in Manchuria from 1941 until transferred to Tinian in March 1944. The troops were battle-hardened veterans of several Manchurian campaigns. Colonel Keishi Ogata commanded the regiment consisting of three 875-man infantry battalions, a 75mm mountain artillery battalion with twelve guns, communication, medical, and engineer companies. This also included a company of twelve light tanks, headquarters support personnel, and an anti-tank platoon. Ogata also had a battalion of the *135th Infantry Regiment* with a troop strength of 900 men. In total, more than 5,000 Japanese Army troops were assigned to the island's defense.

The Navy unit was the *56th Naval Guard Force*. A 1,400-man coastal defense unit supplemented by four construction battalions with a combined strength of 2,000 men. Other naval units totaling 1,000 men included a detachment of the *5th Base Force* and ground elements of seven aviation squadrons.

The Japanese Navy personnel totaled over 4,200 men and were under the immediate command of Captain Oichi Oya. Both Ogata and Oya were outranked by Vice Admiral Kakuji Kakuda, in command of the *1st Air Fleet* headquartered on Tinian. But as the invasion got closer, Kakuda had no air fleet to command. Of the estimated 111 planes based on Tinian's airfields, US airstrikes had destroyed seventy on the ground in early June. By July 24, at the time of the Tinian landing, none of Kakuda's planes were operational.

Kakuda was by Japanese physical standards a hulking figure. He was over six feet tall and weighed more than 200 pounds. He had an unquenchable thirst for liquor and lacked the fortitude to face the odds arrayed against him at Tinian. He was known as a drunk and an extremely unpleasant one, from many accounts.

Nine days before the invasion on July 15, Kakuda and his headquarters group attempted to escape in rubber boats to Aguijan Island and rendezvous with a Japanese submarine. They failed. They tried for five nights in a row with the same results before abandoning the effort on July 21. Kakuda fled with his staff officers to a cave on Tinian's east coast to await their fate.

A Japanese prisoner who later described Kakuda's escape attempt assumed he had committed suicide after the American landing—but that was never verified. Toward the end of the battle for Tinian, one of Kakuda's orderlies led an American patrol to his cave. This patrol was fired on, and two Marines were wounded. Another passing group of Marine pioneers sealed the cave with demolition charges, but it is still unknown whether Kakuda was inside.

Admiral Kakuda had no part in directing any Japanese resistance on Tinian. Colonel Ogata took command of defending the island. He assumed command of both Navy and Army forces. Japanese diaries, later found, showed the friction between the two men. In the *50th Regiment's* artillery battalion, a Japanese soldier wrote: "March 9: The Navy stays in dark buildings and has liberty every night with liquor to drink and fights. On the other hand, we stay in the rain and never get out on any pass—what a difference in discipline.

"June 12: Our anti-aircraft guns manned by the Navy spread black smoke where the enemy planes are not. Not one hit out of over a thousand shots. Our Naval Air Group has taken to its heels.

"June 15: The Naval aviators are thieves. When they ran off to the mountains, they stole Army provisions."

The island's geography dictated Tinian's defenses. It was encircled by coral cliffs that rose from the coastline as part of a limestone plateau that underlined the island. The cliffs were from five to ninety-five feet. Breaks in the cliff were rare and where they did happen were narrow. This left truly little beach space for any invasion force. All along the coastline of Tinian, only four beaches were worthy of the name.

Sunharon Harbor in front of Tinian Town was the most suitable target for an amphibious assault. It had several wide sandy strips. The harbor was mediocre but provided a fair-weather anchorage for ships to load and unload cargo at the two Tinian Town piers.

Colonel Ogata assumed this beach would be the first choice for the Americans. Of the over one-hundred guns in fixed positions on the island—6-inch British naval rifles and 7.7mm heavy machine guns—a third were assigned to the defense of Tinian Town, its beaches, and the airfield at Gurguan Point two miles northwest. Within a two-mile radius of the town were 1,400 men of the *56th Naval Guard Force* and the *135th Infantry Regiment* designated as the mobile counterattack force. Their area of responsibility extended out to Lalo Point on the southernmost part of the island and east to Masalog Point. This made up the "southern sector" of Ogata's defense plan.

The remainder of the island was divided into northeastern and northwestern sectors. The northeast sector had the Ushi Point airfields and a potential landing beach 125 yards wide south of Asiga Point on the island's east coast. Between 500 and 900 Navy personnel were stationed close to the Ushi Airfields. A battalion from the *50th Infantry Regiment* and an engineer group were stationed inland of Asagi Point. In the northwestern sector, there were two narrow strips of beach less than a thousand yards apart. One of them was sixty yards wide and the other twice as long. They were popular with Japanese civilians because the water was swimmable, and the sand was white. Known as the White Beaches—and to the Japanese's great surprise—as the American invasion route.

This sector was defended modestly by a single infantry company and one anti-tank squad, 450 yards northeast of the White Beaches. The gun crews were situated in placements containing a 47mm anti-tank gun, a 37mm anti-tank gun, and two 7.7mm machine guns.

Colonel Ogata established his command post in a cave on Mount Lasso in the center of the northern region, a little over two miles from the beaches on either side of the island. On June 25, he issued orders that said: "the enemy in Saipan can be expected to be planning a landing on Tinian. The area of that landing is estimated to be either Asiga Harbor [on the northeast coast] or Tinian Harbor." Three days later he followed up with a defense forces battle plan which outlined his two contingencies.

(1) In the event the enemy lands at Asiga Bay.

(2) In the event the enemy lands at Tinian Harbor (Sunharon Harbor).

Colonel Ogata issued a plan for the "Guidance of Battle" on July 7. He ordered his men to be prepared for the landings at Asiga Bay and Tinian Town and for a counterattack if the Americans invaded across the White Beaches.

According to his battle plan, in each of the three sectors, commanders were to destroy the enemy at the beach but also be prepared to shift two-thirds of their forces elsewhere. His reserve force was to maintain fortified positions and counterattack points while maintaining anti-aircraft observation and fire in the area. The mobile counterattack force had to rapidly advance to the landings depending on the attack and situation. In the event of a successful landing, his forces would "counterattack to the water and destroy the enemy on beaches with one blow, especially where time prevents quick movement of forces within the island."

If things went badly, they would fall back onto prepared positions in the southern part of the islands and defend each position to the death.

Many of these orders were contradictory and others were impossible to execute. But despite the odds against them—without air or sea support and confronted by three heavily armed divisions only three miles away on Saipan—the Japanese fighting spirit had not been broken by over forty days of heavy bombardment.

In the *50th Infantry Regiment*, a Japanese soldier wrote in his diary on June 30: "We spent over twenty days under unceasing enemy bombardment and air raids but have suffered only minor losses. Everyone from the commanding officer to the lowest private is full of fighting spirit. How exalted are the gallant figures of the Force Commander, the Battalion Commander, and their subordinates who have endured this violent artillery and air bombardment."

WHITE BEACH SELECTION

The selection of northwestern beaches was considered the key to success in the Tinian operation. While credit for this decision has been debated, General Schmidt later wrote on the issue: "many high-ranking officers had asked who originated the plan. While the 4th Division was under my command and before the Mariana's campaign, my planning officer Colonel Evans Carlson made a plan, and probably this plan was turned into V Amphibious Corps."

Colonel Gooderham McCormick, the division's intelligence officer who later became the mayor of Philadelphia, agreed with this assessment. He wrote, "Evans Carlson was the man who planned that landing. He told me all about that Tinian plan before he was wounded on June 22 on Saipan."

General Graves Erskine, the V Amphibious Corps chief of staff, minimized Carlson's role. In an interview, he said, "If there were plans, and I presume there were, none of them were available to me and my staff."

Historian Ronald Spector wrote in his Pacific War history book that General Holland Smith had forced the issue. Rear

Admiral Hill and General Smith proposed using the two White Beaches for the assault, but Admiral Turner vetoed the proposal and told Rear Admiral Hill to plan for a landing near Tinian Town. While Hill reluctantly complied, he ordered part of his staff to continue working on the White Beaches plan. Smith and Hill tried one more time to change Admiral Turner's mind, but he still stubbornly refused to reconsider.

In an exchange characteristic of General Holland Smith and Admiral Turner, Turner said, "you are not going to land on the white beaches. I will not let you land there."

"Oh yes, you will," General Smith said. "You will let me land any goddamn place I tell you to."

Admiral Turner was now upset and adamant. "I'm telling you that it cannot be done. It is absolutely impossible."

General Smith said, "How do you know it's impossible? Are you just so goddamn scared that some of your boats will get hurt?"

This exchange did not change Admiral Turner's mind. So, Hill took the matter to Turner's superior, Admiral Spruance. Spruance liked the White Beaches idea but did not want to overrule Turner—an amphibious warfare expert. After a conference with Turner and his subordinate commanders was arranged on board the flagship. All present spoke in favor of a White Beaches assault. Spruance later turned to Turner, where Turner calmly announced he now also favored the White Beaches.

Admiral Turner later wrote of the incident, "before the reconnaissance of July 11th was available, I had already decided to accept the White Beaches unless the reconnaissance reports were unfavorable."

To quote John F. Kennedy: "Victory has many fathers, but defeat is an orphan."

GENERAL CLIFTON CATES

Clifton Cates was commissioned in 1917. The native Tennessean was sent off to France with the 6th Marines in World War I. He had an outstanding service record in five major engagements of the Great War. He returned to the United States as a well-decorated young officer after his tour in the occupation of Germany.

One of his first early assignments after the war was as an aid to Major General Commandant George Barnett. During his over thirty-seven years as a Marine, Cates was one of the few officers who had commanded a platoon, company, battalion, regiment, and division in combat. At the start of the Korean War, he was the 19th Commandant of the Marine Corps.

His assignments during the interwar years consisted of a combination of staff assignments, and a tour as battalion commander of the 4th Marines at the time in Shanghai. He took command of the 1st Marines in May 1942.

General Cates commanded the 1st Marines in the Guadalcanal landings. After he returned to the US, he was promoted to brigadier general. He then returned to the Pacific War in mid-1944 and took command of the 4th Marine Division on July 12th in time for the Tinian operation, succeeding General Schmidt who had assumed command of the entire V Amphibious Corps. He also led the Iwo Jima assault and was decorated at the end of the fighting with his second Distinguished Service Medal.

Part of his citation that accompanied the medal read: "For repeatedly disregarding his own personal safety. Major General Cates traversed his own front lines daily to rally tired and depleted units. By showing his undaunted valor, tenacious perseverance, and staunch leadership in the face of overwhelming odds, he constantly inspired his stouthearted Marines to heroic efforts during the critical phase of the campaign."

On January 1, 1948, General Cates took over command of the Marine Corps until December 31, 1951, when he reverted to the three stars of a lieutenant general and began a second tour as Commandant of the Marine Corps school at Quantico, Virginia.

General Cates retired from the Marine Corps on June 30, 1954. He died on June 4, 1970, aged 76.

NAPALM: A NEW WEAPON

In 1944 Army Air Corps personnel at Eglin Air Force Base near Fort Walton Beach, Florida, created a new weapon. Known as a "firebomb" and first strategically used near the island of Pohnpei to the southeast of Tinian in February 1944.

The ingredients comprised gasoline, diesel oil, and the metallic salt used in soap manufacturing. Mixed with petroleum fuels, the salt created an incendiary jelly that clung to any surface and burned into a scorching flame. This concoction would be forever known as "napalm." It could be dropped in belly or wing tanks attached to an aircraft's underside and was fired by an igniter on contact with the ground.

Five days before the Tinian landing on July 19, Navy Lieutenant Commander Louis Wang arrived on Saipan carrying a small supply of napalm powder and a film made at Eglin showing this new bomb's potency. It showed P-47 Thunderbolts making the low-level drops after diving from 2,000 feet.

This film so impressed General Schmidt and Rear Admiral Hill that Hill instantly radioed Admiral Nimitz in Hawaii and requested 8,500 pounds of the powder. Hill also ordered trial raids on Tinian by the P-47 pilots of the Army's 318th Air Group—using the powder and detonators they had on hand.

These trials were not remarkable. Their purpose was to burn off wooded areas that were previously resistant to thermite and white phosphorus. The napalm scorched the trees but left the foliage only partially burned. The problem was the wood itself—Ironwood—was virtually indestructible.

Another problem was the napalm mixture. Wang had brought the wrong formula. They tried to use Japanese aviation gasoline but that gave it too much fire effect. Then they used Japanese motor gas and oil with the napalm powder, and that was when it became successful.

Many P-47 pilots were uncomfortable with the napalm missions. They dropped their tanks at low altitudes—sometimes less than forty-five feet—and were vulnerable to ground fire. They were also unimpressed with the effectiveness of these "firebombs" and much of their incendiary effect was wasted in an excessive upward flash. At that time, napalm had a noticeably short burning time—less than two minutes.

One hundred and forty-seven firebombs were used during the Tinian campaign. Ninety-one of them contained the napalm mixture. While they were most effective in clearing cane fields, General Cates later wrote: "the first morning they put it down, I went to the front line and those planes came in over our heads maybe a hundred feet in the air.

"They released their napalm bombs right over our heads and less than 300 yards in front of us. It was devastating and particularly so to the morale of the Japanese. I didn't feel too comfortable sitting there. I figured some of them might drop short."

Each of those bombs cleared an area of over 150 feet and left behind charred bodies of Japanese troops in some cases.

Most Marines were impressed, and infantry commanders sought napalm for their flamethrower tanks.

Napalm was also widely used to support ground troops in the Philippines in 1944. In one Luzon operation, over 200 fighter planes saturated an area with napalm. The usually stoic Japanese fled into the open, making themselves easy targets to pick off.

Napalm was also used in firebombing Japanese cities and the pre-invasion efforts to soften up Iwo Jima's defenses. On January 31, 1945, Seventh Air Force Liberator Bombers began a sixteen-day daytime campaign. Over 600 tons of bombs were dropped, and 1,100 drums of napalm were used in a futile effort to burn off camouflage from defensive positions and gun emplacements.

A Marine intelligence official later wrote, "the main effect of the long bombardment of Iwo was to cause the enemy to build more elaborate underground defenses."

PREPARATORY STRIKES

There were no easy battles in the Pacific War. But there was less concern among the American military about the outcome of Tinian than in almost any other major operation of the war. Admiral Spruance described it as "one of the most brilliantly conceived and executed amphibious operations of the war." General Holland Smith called it the "perfect amphibious operation."

This assault took place under optimal success conditions. The small Japanese garrison on the island had no hope of resupply, relief, victory, or escape. Just three miles away and across the narrow Saipan channel were three battle-tested veteran American divisions—50,000 men—prepared for the inevitable invasion. After a seven-week bombardment from sea, air, and the big guns on Saipan, Tinian had been relentlessly pounded day and night.

Marine General James Underhill, who later became the island's military commander at the end of the battle, wrote: "The state of these people was indescribable. They had no possessions except rags on their backs. After two months of intense bombardment, many suffered from shell shock. They had lived on nothing but scant rations for six weeks and for the past week had nothing to eat.

"They'd been cut off from their water supply for a week and only had what rainwater they could collect in bowls and cans. Hundreds of them were wounded, and some were gangrenous. Syphilis, dysentery, pneumonia, and tuberculosis were common. They needed food, water, shelter, medical care, and sanitation."

On June 11, the bombardment began four days after Saipan's invasion when carrier planes from Task Force 58 launched a three-day pummeling of the principal Mariana Islands. After a fighter sweep on the first day, 225 Grumman Hellcats destroyed 150 Japanese aircraft, America's control over the islands' skies was secured.

After the raid, a Japanese soldier garrisoned on Saipan wrote in his diary: "for over two hours the planes ran amok. They finally left leisurely during the inaccurate anti-aircraft fire. All we could do was watch helplessly and die."

Over the next two days, the bombers hit the islands in the shipping area with zero let-up. Battleships from Task Force 58 joined in the bombardment from long range on June 13. Their firing was later considered ineffective and misdirected at soft targets rather than the concealed gun positions circling the island.

During the next six weeks, the effort to destroy Tinian's defenses escalated. Navy Task Force 52, on June 18, added its firepower to the mission. More airstrikes involving carrier planes and Army P-47s were ordered. Starting on June 28 until Jig Day on July 24, massed artillery battalions fired from Saipan's southern shore poured thousands of tons of artillery onto the island. By July 15, thirteen battalions were engaged in the mission, firing a total of 160 guns—105mm and 155mm around the clock.

While the exact effect from the artillery assault on Saipan will never be known, a young major at the time serving as the operations officer in the 4th Marines during the Tinian campaign later wrote: "I remember going by one of the Japanese machine gun crews. They'd been trying to get to a firing position and were caught by the artillery barrage. They were laid out just like a 'school solution.' Each man carried his own particular portion of the gun crew's equipment. And that was where they died."

In the two weeks from June 26 to July 9, cruisers, *Birmingham*, *Montpelier*, and the *Indianapolis* hit the islands daily. Their fire was supplemented by battleships: *Tennessee*, *Colorado*, and *California*. Joined in by the cruisers *Cleveland*, *New Orleans*, and *Louisville*, and sixteen destroyers and dozens of other supporting vessels. They fired various ordinances ranging from 40mm and rocket barrages to white phosphorus targeted at the wooden areas around the Japanese command post on Mount Lasso.

AERIAL RECONNAISSANCE

Before the invasion of Tinian, an intensive reconnaissance was underway. The first aerial photographs of 1944 were acquired back in February when US carrier planes attacked Saipan. More were obtained in April and May by photo planes based at Eniwetok. These early photographs were scarce and of little use to the invasion planners. The quality was poor, and many were taken at angles that distorted the terrain.

These problems hindered the Saipan planners, but on Tinian, it was another story. Perhaps no other Pacific island had become so familiar to the assault forces because of such thorough photography and mapping prior to the landings.

Much of the familiarization came from first-hand observation by battalion, division, and regimental commanders who used observation planes to conduct their own reconnaissance of the Tinian beaches and inland terrain.

Colonel Justice M. Chambers, the commander of the 3/25 Marines later wrote of his pre-invasion visit to the island: "A naval aviator named Lieutenant Commander Muller had sent a lot of roving orders. He brought his flight of three Liberators to Saipan. I thought it was a good idea to take my company commanders and overfly the beaches we were going to use. So, the 3rd Battalion group took the flight and many other battalions followed suit.

"We took off from Saipan, and of course the minute you're airborne, you're right over Tinian. I talked it over with Muller and told him that the last beach we would overfly would be the one we were going to hit. I said, 'let's take a look at some of the other beaches first and then fly over through the interior.' After we made passes over several of the beaches. I stood up in a blister where I could see my officers. We had the bomb bays open and were looking down. After flying around for twenty minutes, we made a big loop and then came back over the beaches where we were going to land. I'm glad we did because we spotted mines in the water which the Navy UDT teams later disposed of.

"We zoomed in on Mount Lasso, the only mountain on Tinian. This island was just one big cane field, and Mount Lasso was directly ahead of our beaches. Muller pulled out, and I saw white things zipping by the outside of our plane. I fought to keep my stomach down because a fast elevator is too much for me. I asked, 'what's that?'

"Mueller said, 'twenty millimeter. Where do you want to go now?'

"'Saipan. There aren't any foxholes up here,' I said."

The photographic coverage of Tinian, along with documents, prisoners captured on Saipan, and other intelligence, allowed US forces to become as familiar with Japanese strength on Tinian as Colonel Ogata.

HEROES OF TINIAN

Private First Class Robert Lee Wilson was born on May 21, 1920 and grew up on his parents' farm with seven siblings. He enlisted in the Marine Corps in the fall of 1941 and served in the 2nd Battalion, 6th Marines, 2nd Marine Division during action against enemy Japanese forces on Tinian Island on August 4, 1944.

As one in a group of Marines advancing through heavy underbrush to neutralize isolated points of resistance, Private First Class Wilson advanced ahead of his companions toward a pile of rocks where Japanese troops were supposedly hiding. He was fully aware of the danger involved. He moved forward while the rest of the squad armed with automatic rifles closed together in the rear. An enemy grenade landed in the middle of the group. Private First Class Wilson cried a warning to the men and unhesitatingly threw himself on the grenade—heroically sacrificing his own life so that others might live and fulfill the mission. He was awarded the Medal of Honor for his exceptional valor, courageous loyalty, and unwavering devotion to duty in the face of great peril.

Private Joseph W. Ozbourn was both in Herrin Illinois in 1919. He enlisted in the Marine Corps on 30 Oct 1943 and served with the 1st Battalion, 23rd Marines, in the 4th Marine Division, during the battle for enemy held Tinian Island on July 30, 1944

Private Ozbourn was a member of a platoon assigned the mission of clearing remaining Japanese troops from dugouts of pillboxes along the tree line. Private Osborne was flanked by two men and moving forward to throw a hand grenade into a dugout when a terrific blast from the entrance wounded the four men and himself. Unable to throw the grenade into the dugout and with no place to hurl it without endangering his comrades. Private Ozbourn unhesitatingly grasped the grenade close to his body and fell on it, sacrificing his own life to absorb the full impact of the explosion—saving his comrades. For his unwavering loyalty and great personal valor in gallantly giving his life for his country, Private Ozbourn too was awarded the Medal of Honor.

The destroyer USS *Ozbourn*, named in his honor, was christened by the widow Ozbourns on 22 Dec 1945 and was launched out of Boston.

* * *

Building a relationship with my readers is one of the best things about writing. I occasionally send out emails with details on new releases and special offers. If you'd like to join my free readers group and never miss a new release, just go to daniel-wrinn.com and you can sign up for the list.

REFERENCES

Information available for researching the World War II Pacific Theater is vast. I've listed my main reference sources below. Websites, newspaper articles, and even History Channel documentaries also contributed to my research.

Chapin, Captain John C. "Breaching the Marianas - United States Marine Corps." U.S. Marine Corps Reserve (RET), 1994.

Chen, C. Peter. "Mariana Islands Campaign and the Great Turkey Shoot." World War II Database. Lava Development, LLC, 2004.

Chen, C. Peter. "Palau Islands and Ulithi Islands Campaign," World War II Database. Lava Development, LLC, 2007.

Denfeld, D. Colt, and Eugene L. Rasor. "Hold the Marianas: The Japanese Defense of the Islands." *The Journal of Military History*, 1997.

Drea, Edward J. "An Allied Interpretation of the Pacific War." 1998.

Drea, Edward J. Essay. In *In the Service of the Emperor: Essays on the Imperial Japanese Army*. Lincoln, Neb.: University of Nebraska Press, 2003.

Dull, Paul s. *A Battle History of the Imperial Japanese Navy, 1941-1945*. Annapolis: Naval Institute Press, 1978.

Dyer, George Carroll. *The Amphibians Came to Conquer: the Story of Admiral Richmond Kelly Turner*. Washington, D.C, Dept. of the Navy,: United States Government Printing Office – via Hyperwar Foundation, 1973.

Gailey, Harry A. *The Liberation of Guam, 21 July-10 August 1944*. Novato, CA: Presidio, 1988.

Gailey, Harry A. *Peleliu, 1944*. Annapolis, MD: Nautical & Aviation Pub. Co. of America, 1983. ISBN 0-933852-41-X.

Gnam, Carl. "Marine Fight for Tinian: A squabble between a general and an admiral led to 'the most perfect amphibious operation of the Pacific War.'" Warfare History Network, June 16, 2020.

Goldberg, Harold J. *D-Day in the Pacific The Battle of Saipan*. Bloomington: Indiana University Press, 2007.

Guillaume, Marine. "Napalm in US Bombing Doctrine and Practice, 1942-1975." Sciences Po portal, December 10, 2016.

Hallas, James H. *The Devil's Anvil: the Assault on Peleliu*. Westport, CT: Praeger, 1994.

Harwood, Richard. "A Close Encounter: The Marine Landing on Tinian." 1994.

Hoffman, Major Carl W., USMC. *Saipan: the Beginning of the End*. Washington, D.C.: Historical Division, U.S. Marine Corps, 1950.

Hoffman, Major Carl W., USMC. *The Seizure of Tinian:* Washington, DC: Historical Division, Headquarters, U.S. Marine Corps, 1951.

O'Brien, Cyril J. "Liberation: Marines in the Recapture of Guam", Marine Corps Historical Center, United States Marine Corps, 1994.

O'Brien, Francis. *Battling for Saipan*. New York: Ballantine Books, 2003.

Rottman, Gordon L. *Saipan & Tinian 1944: Piercing the Japanese Empire*. Oxford: Osprey, 2004.

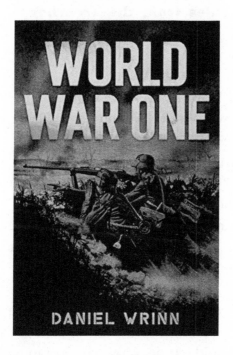

WORLD WAR ONE: WWI HISTORY TOLD FROM THE
TRENCHES, SEAS, SKIES, AND DESERT OF A WAR TORN
WORLD

"Compelling . . . the kind of book that brings history alive." – Reviewer
**Dive into the incredible history of WWI with these
gripping stories.**

With a unique and fascinating glimpse into the lesser-
known stories of the War to End All Wars, this riveting book
unveils four thrilling stories from the trenches, seas, skies, and
desert of a war-torn world. From one captain's death-defying
mission to smuggle weapons for an Irish rebellion to heroic
pilots and soldiers from all corners of the globe, these stories

shed light on real people and events from one of the greatest conflicts in human history.

- **WWI: Tales from the Trenches**, a sweeping and eerily realistic narrative which explores the struggles and endless dangers faced by soldiers in the trenches during the heart of WWI
- **Broken Wings**, a powerful and heroic story about one pilot after he was shot down and spent 72 harrowing days on the run deep behind enemy lines
- **Mission to Ireland**, which explores the devious and cunning plan to smuggle a ship loaded with weapons to incite an Irish rebellion against the British
- And **Journey into Eden**, a fascinating glimpse into the lesser-known battles on the harsh and unforgiving Mesopotamian Front

World War I reduced Europe's mightiest empires to rubble, killed twenty million people, and cracked the foundations of our modern world. In its wake, empires toppled, monarchies fell, and whole populations lost their national identities.

Each of these stories brings together unbelievable real-life WWI history, making them perfect for casual readers and history buffs alike. If you want to peer into the past and unearth the incredible stories of the brave soldiers who risked everything, then this book is for you.

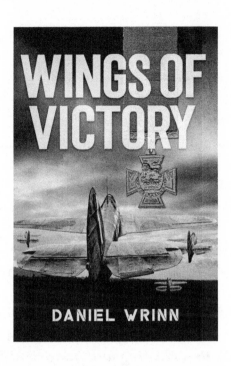

WINGS OF VICTORY: WORLD WAR II ADVENTURES IN A WAR-
TORN EUROPE

"Historical fiction with a realistic twist." – Reviewer

Thrilling World War II adventures like you've never seen them before.

As the Nazis invade Europe on a campaign for total domination, a brutal war begins to unfold which will change the course of the world forever—and John Archer finds himself caught in the middle of it. When this amateur pilot joins the Allied war effort and is tasked with a series of death-defying missions which place him deep into German-occupied territory, his hair-raising adventures will help decide the fate of Europe.

In **War Heroes**, John is caught up in the devastating Nazi invasion of France while on vacation. Teaming up with ambulance driver Barney, John will need his amateur pilot skills and more than a stroke of luck to pull off the escape of the century.

In **Bombs Over Britain**, the Nazis have a plan which could change the course of the entire war . . . unless Archer can stop them. Air-dropped into Belgium on a top-secret mission, Archer must retrieve vital intelligence and make it out alive. But that's easier said than done when the Gestapo are closing in.

And in **Desert Scout**, Archer finds himself stranded beneath the scorching Libyan sun and in a race against time to turn the tide of the war in North Africa. But with the Luftwaffe and the desert vying to finish him off, can he make it out alive?

Packed with action and filled to the brim with suspense, these thrilling stories combine classic adventures with a riveting and historical World War II setting, making it ideal for history buffs and casual readers. If you're a fan of riveting war fiction novels, WW2 aircraft, and the war for the skies, Archer's next adventure will keep you on the edge of your seat.

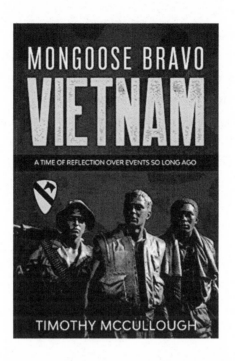

MONGOOSE BRAVO: VIETNAM: A TIME OF REFLECTION OVER
EVENTS SO LONG AGO

"A frank, real, memoir" – Reviewer

**Uncover the gritty, real-life story of a Vietnam
combat veteran.**

With an engaging and authentic retelling of his experiences as an infantry soldier of the B Co., 1/5th 1st Cavalry
Division in the Vietnam War, this gripping account details the
life and struggles of war in a strange and foreign country.

What started as a way of bringing closure to a grieving
mother morphed into a memoir, covering the author's deployment, duty, and eventual return to the United States after the
end of the war. Imbued with the emotion that he felt during
this conflicted time, along with letters and journal entries from
decades ago, this memoir is a testament to the sacrifice that
these brave men and women made fighting on foreign soil.

Recounting the tragedies of war and the chaos of combat as an infantry soldier, in the words of the author: "We lived, and fought as a unit, covering each other's backs. Most came home to tell their own stories, many didn't."

If you like gripping, authentic accounts of life and combat during the Vietnam War, then you won't want to miss Mongoose Bravo: Vietnam: A Time of Reflection Over Events So Long Ago.

ABOUT THE AUTHOR

Daniel Wrinn writes Military History & War Stories. A US Navy veteran and avid history buff, Daniel lives in the Utah Wasatch Mountains. He writes every day with a view of the snow capped peaks of Park City to keep him company. You can join his readers group and get notified of new releases, special offers, and free books here:

www.danielwrinn.com